BRJC
'58

Animals of the Rain Forest

By Dana Sadan

The Child's World

www.childsworld.com

Published in the United States of America by The Child's World®
1980 Lookout Drive • Mankato, MN 56003-1705
800-599-READ • www.childsworld.com

ACKNOWLEDGMENTS

The Child's World® : Mary Berendes, Publishing Director

Produced by Shoreline Publishing Group LLC
President / Editorial Director: James Buckley, Jr.
Designer: Tom Carling, carlingdesign.com
Cover Art: Slimfilms
Assistant Editor: Jim Gigliotti

Photo Credits:
Cover: Main and lemurs: Photos.com; frog: iStock.
Interior: AP/Wide World: 28, 29; Corbis: 22, 26; Dreamstimes.com
(photographers listed): 16, Asdf1 7, Michael Guser 27, Phil Morley
11, Batman2000 13; DK Picture Library: 17; istock: 14, 19, 20;
Photos.com: 5, 9, 10, 12, 15, 18, 22, 24, 25. Maps on 6 and 8 by Robert
Prince.

LIBRARY OF CONGRESS CATALOG-IN-PUBLICATION DATA

Sadan, Dana.
  Animals of the rain forest / by Dana Sadan.
    p. cm. — (Reading rocks!)
  Includes bibliographical references and index.
  ISBN 978-1-60253-094-2 (library bound : alk. paper)
 1. Rain forest animals—Juvenile literature. I. Title. II. Series.

QL112.S24 2008
591.734—dc22

                                              2008004387

CONTENTS

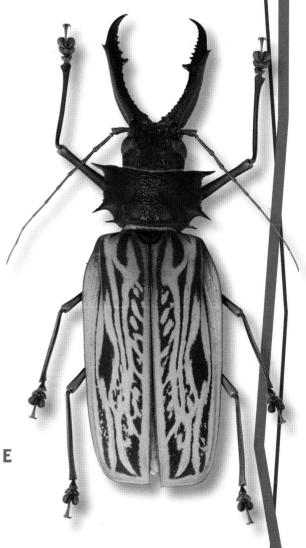

WHAT'S A Rain Forest?

Imagine walking in green twilight through a forest of giant trees. Their leafy branches block sunlight from reaching the ground below. Imagine a damp place drenched with as much as 32 feet (10 m) of rain per year. It's a place where the temperature hardly changes. It stays between 70 and 90° F (21 and 32° C) all year round. Where are you? You're in a **rain forest**!

Rain forests are important **ecosystems**. About half of all the world's animals live in rain forests.

Did you know that nearly half of the world's medicines come from rain-forest plants? And take a deep breath— some of the air you just breathed is thanks in part to the rain forests.

Before we meet some of the weird and wild animals that live in the world's rain forests, let's learn a little more about these warm, wet, and important places.

Rain forests (dark green) cover about six percent (or 6 of every 100 square miles) of Earth's land surface.

Almost all rain forests are found near the **equator**. The equator is an imaginary line around the center of the Earth. Places near the equator have warm weather all year round.

The world's largest areas of rain forests are in Central and South

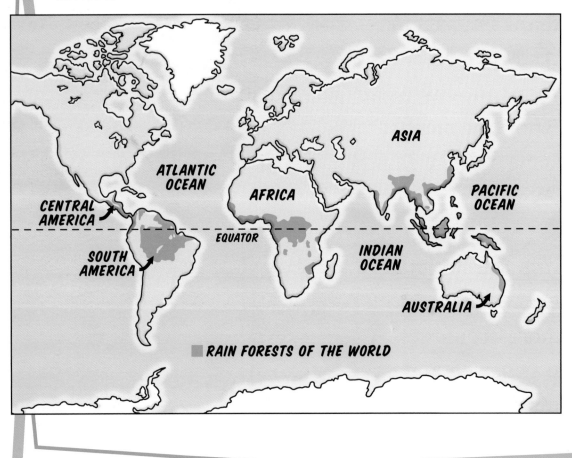

ASIA

ATLANTIC OCEAN

AFRICA

PACIFIC OCEAN

CENTRAL AMERICA

EQUATOR

SOUTH AMERICA

INDIAN OCEAN

AUSTRALIA

RAIN FORESTS OF THE WORLD

America. Rain forests can also be found in Asia, Africa, and Australia. The Amazon rain forest in Brazil is the largest. It's almost as big as Australia!

The Amazon rain forest is located along both sides of the mighty Amazon River. The forest covers an enormous area of Brazil and stretches into other countries.

This photo shows just a tiny part of the Amazon rain forest that runs through Peru.

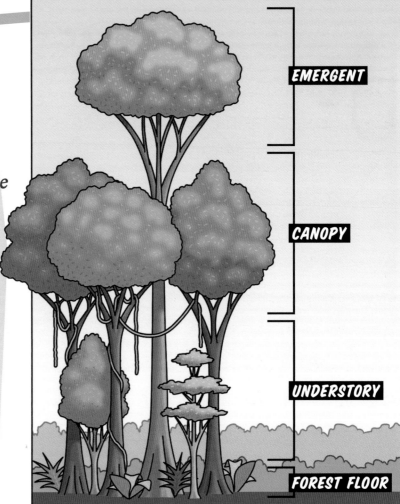

EMERGENT

CANOPY

UNDERSTORY

FOREST FLOOR

Think of the rain forest as an apartment building. Each "floor" is home to different kinds of animals.

The rain forest's understory is sometimes called the "lower canopy."

There are four main layers of plants within a rain forest. Starting from the top down, they are the **emergent** layer, the **canopy**, the understory, and the forest floor. Each layer is home to a huge number of living creatures.

The emergent layer has the tallest trees, some standing as high as 200 feet (61 m). Many birds live in this high, sunny layer.

Most rain-forest life is found in the canopy layer. This can be 100 to 150 feet (30 to 46 m) above the ground. The canopy is like a huge platform covered with leaves, moss, and flowering plants called **epiphytes** (EP-uh-fites).

Some animals of the rain forest, such as this green tree frog, have the brightest colorings in the animal world.

The canopy has hundreds of types of birds, insects, reptiles, and mammals. Some live in the high trees year-round, never touching the ground.

You know how your bathroom gets hot and steamy during a shower? That's humid!

The trees of the understory only grow to be about 12 feet (about 4 m) high. This layer is home to animals that must live closer to the forest floor, where they can find food and water.

The forest floor is very dark, hot, and **humid**. Very little light filters down through the branches above. Wherever light *does* reach the floor, life rises. Animals find homes amid the lush plants.

Jaguars like this one live on the forest floor.

Sometimes things fall from the canopy layer (such as dead leaves, branches, and even animals). These things are used as food by the plants and animals on the forest floor. Most of the forest's smaller animals live on the floor. Animals that hunt them (called **predators**) live here, too.

At every layer of this amazing world, creatures live, play, grow, and eat. Let's take a trip to the rain forest and meet some of them.

Thick moss, dark-green ferns, and vines of all sorts shelter animals on the floor of the rain forest.

2

RAIN FOREST
Animals

The rain forest is a busy and dangerous place. At every minute of every day, animals are being hunted by other animals. Big cats, eagles, and snakes are some of the most common rain-forest predators.

The jaguar is the rain-forest ruler. This crafty hunter can sneak up on its food almost without a sound. An adult jaguar weighs about 120 pounds (54 kg) and hunts turtles, **tapirs**, and deer.

The harpy eagle is a flying hunting machine. This huge bird weighs about 12 pounds (5 kg) and has a large, hooked beak. Harpy eagles hunt monkeys and smaller animals.

The rain forest is home to many snakes. Some of the most dangerous are **constrictors**. These snakes surprise their **prey** and wrap quickly around them. They squeeze the prey until it stops breathing. Pythons and boas are constrictors.

A hooked beak and sharp claws make the harpy eagle a deadly hunter.

OPPOSITE PAGE
Emerald tree boas like this one grow to be about 7 feet (2 m) long.

Army ants swarm over the forest floor in search of food.

Even tiny creatures in the rain forest can be dangerous! Army ants travel in groups of more than 200,000. They swarm and attack anything that crosses their path—especially other insects. Certain army ants have huge jaws that can bite through skin.

Many of the rain forest's insects, spiders, and snakes have poisonous bites or stings. This helps them catch and kill their prey. Other animals trap their food. Huge bird-eating spiders spin webs to catch their big prey—birds!

Perhaps the biggest rain-forest pests are bloodsucking botflies. These flies lay their eggs on mammals, including people. When the **larvae** hatch, they burrow under the host's skin and cause painful itching.

Green scarab beetles (above) and bird-eating spiders can only be found in rain forests.

Thousands of types of spiders live in rain forests. The world's largest spider is the goliath bird-eating spider, which lives in South America. This spider would cover most of a large dinner plate!

Dart frogs have very bright colors. This warns predators to stay away!

Some rain-forest insects and frogs produce a poison in their bodies that makes them "sickening" to eat. Their bold colors tell predators to leave them alone. Tasting bad keeps them safe!

The most famous poison-producers are dart frogs. There are many kinds of dart frogs, and all are less than three inches (8 cm) long. They live in certain streams and rivers in South America, and eat crickets, flies, and ants. Dart frogs produce a strong poison under their skin. This stops predators from eating them. Some native peoples use the frogs' poison on the tips of their hunting darts. That's how the frogs got their name!

The Queen Alexandra's birdwing butterfly is the largest butterfly in the world. Its **wingspan** is up to 12 inches (30 cm). The butterfly lays its eggs on a poisonous plant. The birdwing caterpillars then eat the leaves of the plant. When they grow into butterflies, they are poisonous to predators.

Queen Alexandra's birdwing butterflies live in Papua New Guinea.

Some rain-forest animals avoid becoming prey by imitating other poisonous animals. Some do this by developing markings such as "false eyes" to trick or surprise predators. Others have developed the ability to disappear into the forest. They use camouflage to blend into their surroundings.

The branch is brown, so the chameleon turns that color, too!

The chameleon lizard, for example, firmly grips branches for support with its feet and tail. It stays

hidden on branches by matching its skin to the greens and browns nearby. But if it feels threatened, a chameleon can turn blue or even bright red to scare an enemy away.

Sloths are the slow movers of the rain forest. They are so slow, it might take them a whole day to move from one tree to another! Many creatures, including beetles, mites, and moths have been found to live in a sloth's fur. Algae can grow on a sloth's fur, too. This gives the fur a green tint, helping the animal to blend in with nearby plants.

Sloths use their sharp claws to dig into trees in search of tasty bugs.

Cover your ears if this howler monkey starts making its amazing calls.

Some of the largest animals in the rain forest are **primates**, or monkeys and apes. In South America's rain forests, there are only monkeys. The howler monkey is one of the loudest animals in the world. It gets its name from the roaring voice of the main male of a group. The howler is also the largest primate of the Amazon rain forest.

South America's spider monkeys are the acrobats of the forest. They have strong arms and a tail that can grab like a hand. Spider monkeys can dangle from branches to reach fruit growing in difficult places.

Orangutans are apes that live in the rain forests of southeastern Asia. Their powerful arms and hooked-shaped hands let them swing easily from branch to branch.

This baby orangutan clings to her mother's side as she swings from tree to tree.

Gorillas are found only in the rain forests of Central Africa. Because of their size, these huge apes stay mainly on the forest floor. Gorillas can look scary, but their displays of screaming and beating are just for show. They are mostly gentle giants, and feed on leaves, fruit, and bark.

Some pretty awesome fish live in the many rivers and streams that wind through the rain forest. One famous rain-forest fish is the piranha. It lives in South America's Amazon River.

Piranhas are known for their fierce behavior and sharp teeth. These teeth are tightly packed and are used to bite chunks from their prey's body. Most piranhas bite and quickly leave their prey—alive. But a group of piranhas will sometimes attack a sick animal. When this happens, the animal doesn't have a chance. The snapping piranhas will leave only bones behind.

Not a friendly fish face: Imagine dozens of these attacking all at once!

The pirarucu (peer-ar-uh-KOO) is the largest fish in the Amazon River. At six feet (2 m) long, it has few enemies.

This powerful fish has a special way of breathing. Unlike most fish that must use **gills** to breathe, the pirarucu has a trick. When it has to, a pirarucu can breathe air from the surface through its mouth.

The pirarucu can actually leap out of the water and snatch birds perched too close to the water's edge!

The pirarucu is one of the world's largest freshwater fish.

THE ANIMALS' GREEN Home

3

If you think the animals of the rain forest are wild, wait until you meet some of the plants they live with!

Pitcher plants' leaves grow in the shape of water jugs. The "pitchers" fill with a juice that attracts insects. But once a bug climbs in, it can't escape—and drowns! Over time, the bug rots in the liquid, and the plant absorbs the "bug juice."

The strangler fig grows high on the trunk of a larger tree. It drops strong roots around the trunk of the larger tree to the forest floor. The roots take hold and then, as the strangler fig grows in size, it entwines itself tightly around the host tree. The fig slowly strangles the life out of the larger tree. Over time, the host tree **decomposes**, but the strangler fig remains.

The roots of a strangler fig cover this large tree in South America.

OPPOSITE PAGE
You can see the "jug" part of this pitcher plant.

The butterwort is another predator plant. Its bright flowers attract insects. But once insects land, they get glued to the plant's sticky surface. The insect soon dies and rots, and the plant absorbs the meal.

Another interesting rain-forest plant is the rafflesia (ruh-FLEEZSH-uh), which grows in Asia. With its thick, warty petals and spiky center, the rafflesia boasts the biggest flowers in the world—up to three feet (1 m) across! But these flowers don't smell sweet.

Instead, they smell awful—like rotting meat!

Lianas (lee-AH-nahs) are large, woody vines that grow out of the forest floor and climb up to the canopy. They attach themselves to young trees and grow along with them, or they climb up a taller, older tree. Some lianas grow up to 300 feet (91 m) tall.

From tall tree to dark, dense floor, the rain forest crackles with life. Nowhere else in the world boasts as many amazing animals and interesting plants.

In this picture, you can see how liana vines have grown along another tree to reach the forest canopy.

A Call to Action

Sadly, rain forests are disappearing to make way for people and crops. Struggling or poor farmers, urged by governments to leave overcrowded cities, have taken over large areas of land. They use "slash-and-burn" farming methods. This means they burn the trees to clear areas and enrich the soil for farming. Without the trees, many miles of animal **habitat** are destroyed.

Large areas of rain forests have also been sold to timber and mining businesses. These big companies strip the land of trees and minerals and leave behind a wasteland. Every day, huge areas of forest are lost to this kind of destruction.

It's not too late to save many rain forests, however. Many people have worked hard to slow down the destruction of rain forests. They speak to people around the world and try to show how important rain forests are to all of us. But there is still a lot of work to be done. Perhaps you can get involved with a **conservation** group and help save these amazing forests. The poison dart frog, the orangutan, and even the strangler fig will thank you!

People protest against companies they say are hurting rain-forest areas.

GLOSSARY

canopy   the second-highest layer in a rain forest

conservation   preserving resources for the future

constrictors   snakes that kill their prey by squeezing

decomposes   rots away to turn into soil

ecosystems   locations where plants, animals, land, and weather combine to create a unique lifestyle

emergent   the highest, sunniest layer in a rain forest

epiphytes   plants that grow on other plants

equator   an imaginary line around the middle of the Earth

gills   thin slits on a fish's sides that allow it to take in air from the water

habitat   the type of surroundings in which an animal lives

humid   damp, moist

larvae   young insects that have not changed into their adult forms

predators   animals that hunt and kill other animals

prey   animals that are hunted

primates   a group of animals that includes monkeys, apes, and people

rain forest   a thick forest area that gets at least 100 inches (254 cm) of rain a year

tapirs   a pig-like animal with a flexible snout

wingspan   the distance from wingtip to wingtip

FIND OUT MORE

BOOKS

Does It Always Rain in the Rain Forest?
by Melvin Berger and Gilda Berger (Scholastic, 2002)
Questions and answers that introduce young readers to the
fascinating world of the rain forest.

Rain Forest (DK 24 Hours)
by Helen Sharman (DK Children, 2006)
See how the plants and animals of a rain forest spend an
entire day, from morning to night.

Rain Forests (Magic Tree House Research Guide)
by Will Osborne and Mary Pope Osborne (Random House Books
for Young Readers, 2001)
Jack and Annie of the popular Magic Tree House books guide
readers through the rain forest.

WEB SITES

Visit our Web site for lots of links about rain forests:
www.childsworld.com/links

Note to Parents, Teachers, and Librarians: We routinely check our Web links to
make sure they're safe, active sites—so encourage your readers to check them out!

INDEX

DANA SADAN has been an elementary school teacher for 13 years and has always wanted to write books. She lives in California with her children— Natasha, Mallory, and Sebastian—and a menagerie of animals including a dog, a cat, a beta fish, a bearded dragon, two fire-bellied toads, and two hermit crabs!